Poems, Passages and Lyrics

Searching for Why

KEN WINGATE

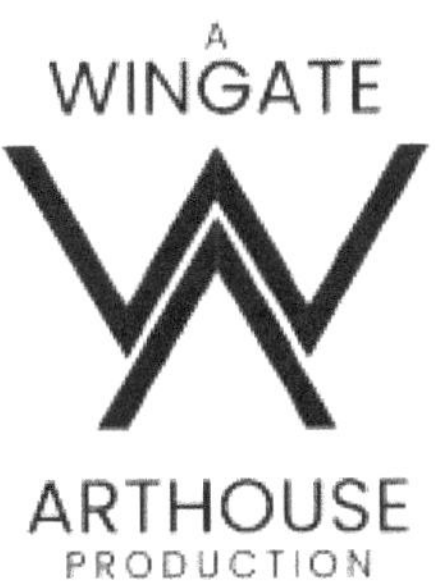

"Art That's Made for the Senses" ™
www.wingatearthouse.com

DEDICATION

iii

To my wife, Judy, who has believed in me and supported
me with all of her heart on this project.

To my two daughters, Elizabeth and Anna, for their
support and love.

FOREWORD

Thank you for allowing me to share my art with you. I do not take that for granted. Enclosed you will find portraits of memories and expressions in words. That is my art. As with all art, that means it is subjective. If everyone loved all the art they read, saw, or heard, there would be no such thing as a "starving artist." But that is not the case.

You may dislike some of my works, maybe even hate some, but I am confident that if you open your heart and mind, you will find many of these works will speak to you. That is my hope. None of us is alone. None of us is an island. We all share hurt, warmth, love, and victories sometimes in our lives. How deep those hurts are or how joyous those victories are depends on who we are inside. So, I hope you will read my works and enjoy those that speak to you.

To provide you with an idea of where I come from in my art, I will share with you a bit of who I am. I lived in thirteen different homes in Virginia and North Carolina by the time I was eighteen. My mom had a wanderlust about her and my dad just followed along. I was the baby of five children, the caboose. I was the one that was not planned for. My mom and dad loved me but I was often left alone to myself. I grew up with insecurities of who I was. I have also struggled with depression my whole life.

Politically, I am an independent moderate with a social conscious leaning. That social conscious leaning comes from my faith. I believe in God through the compassionate teachings of Jesus Christ. I am not ashamed of that but I am ashamed of how the religious right-wing zealots within the churches across the United States are portraying God at the present. They are worshiping a false God of their making, not the compassionate God that Jesus Christ portrayed and taught us about.

Within these pages you will find portraits of life and faith from the core of my passionate and loving heart. They are my truth. I hope they will encourage you to find your truth. Take care of yourself.

Ken

"Poor choices have short term negative consequences. Bad decisions have long term negative consequences. Try to make as few poor choices and even fewer bad decisions in this life and you will do well."

Ken Wingate

Contents

LIFE AND LOVE

SECRETS HELD

In the deepest part of me
Is the darkest part of me
That none shall ever know
That none shall ever see

The secrets held inside that place
The secrets that I hide
Will never see the light of day
Will still be there the day I die

Don't judge me harsh with pompous minds
Don't judge me in the least
For within every one of us
Are the secrets that we keep

You can lie to all you know
You can lie to even you
But the secrets are still there
So, none will know yours too

I HAD A THOUGHT

I had a thought
  but it got lost
I had a dream
  go up in steam
I had a wish
  so rudely dissed
I had a hope
  go up in smoke
I had a laugh
  back in my past
I had my fun
  then had to run
I had it all
  then came the fall
Still I am here
  and without fear
I will press on
  to a new dawn
I keep looking for
  an open door
No need to quit
  or have a fit
One day I'll find
  that special rhyme

LIFE OR DEATH

It is said that we bring life or death
to everyone we come in contact with.
Think about that.
Be aware.
Never underestimate the smallest choices
you make in your life.
One single choice can end up good or bad
and could live with you -
until the end of your days.
Every day, everything you do, affects someone.
Even a simple or slight recognition to a passing soul
acknowledges to them they are not alone.
During times of extreme darkness,
the slightest glimmer of hope
can sustain a person's soul.
None of us are perfect, we all falter.
But we should always strive to do good,
to do what is right;
lest when we ourselves need a breath of life
we find only death around us.

IT'S CRUSHING

It's crushing.
I know.
You meet someone
and it seems good.
You get along
and have some fun.
Your hearts
grow close.
It seems
so right.
And then
you realize.
You love them
more than they
love you.
It just
doesn't work.
It's crushing.

EVIL AND HATRED SURROUND ME

Evil and hatred surround me
    hoping to destroy the light within
Though its strength has grown immensely
    I hold strong and refuse to give in

Where did such evil come from
    where did it gain all its might
How can so many be deaf and blind
    and not recognize wrong from right

It's disheartening to hear all the lies
    be received as if they are true
The hardened hearts have taken hold
    their followers have increased too

Who will stand in these troublesome times
    and say enough damage is done
We the people are still the strength
    of this nation we have built upon

We must rise and claim what is ours
    our numbers are greater – so fight
Against the wicked bent to oppress us
    with courage and all of our might

THE PARADOX OF LIFE

If I had known then
what I know now,
I would still know more now
than I did then.
So is the paradox of life.

WON'T YOU STAY

I know that the past
Has not been too kind and it's hurting you
I see all the pain
Cuts run so deep have torn you in two
Now I'm standing here
Waiting for you to see
There's still life to live
If you'll let the past be

Won't you stay, say that you will
Hold me, love me until
Can't you see how love is right here
Stay now, you've nothing to fear
Won't you stay

One minute you say
You know you love me and that it can work
The next you break down
And say that you just do not know for sure
The time that we've shared
It has brought us so close
The love that you want
Is right here with me

Won't you stay, say that you will
Hold me, love me until
Can't you see how love is right here
Stay now, you've nothing to fear
Won't you stay

POSE THE ROSES

She sees life through
    the beauty of her creations
The expressions provided
    with such visual emotions
The colors so vibrant and alive
    speak what words cannot
With such care and tenderness
    she sets out to plot
How each creation speaks true
    of the sentiments conveyed
With the colors carefully chosen
    wanting only the truth portrayed
The reds are for true romantic love
    the whites for innocence and purity
The pinks for gentleness, grace, and joy
    the purples for infatuation and sincerity
The yellows speak loud of friends and caring
    the oranges enthusiasm, passion, and desire
The blues entice an illusion of mystery
    the greens a promise of a prosperous life
She will carefully pose the roses to show
    just what the giver desires to declare
To the recipient of such beauty and awe
    and the depth to which their lives do share

WRITING

Writing is therapy
    writing is a curse
It can bring out your best
    or expose your worst
You put it out in the world
    for others to see
They may tear it to pieces
    or love it wholly
But you still sit and write
    because that's what you do
And hope it might connect
    for those seeking to
Know they are not alone
    in this world that we live
They can find peace in reading
    in writing such as this
You are not alone...

BE A REALIST

I am a realist
Objective by nature
Neither positive or negative
I have a need to be sure

Being objective is relevant
In this world that we live
Deception is spreading like fire
It's all relative

Being a realist
With eyes wide open
Is a proper balance
Keeping sanity within

So be real with life
And it will be real with you
See the lies all around
Always seek what's true

Be a realist
Be objective

LOVE CANNOT HATE

Love cannot hate
    it can be displeased
It can have regrets
    it can surely grieve
It can feel pain
    when it has lost
It can deeply weep
    when suffering a loss
It can get angry
    by unjust acts
It can scream out loud
    from a hurtful past
It can be hurt
    by words said wrong
It can shed a tear
    from a memory or song
Love can feel
    emotions intense
As it should always
    without resent
But love cannot hate
    when it's true and sure
For hate has no place
    in a love that is pure

I JUST WANT TO SCREAM

These days I just want to scream
    I just want to close my eyes
The nightmare that is right now
    The chaos and flagrant lies
Watching democracy fall
    Brick by brick tearing it down
The hate rising up from hell
    Sadness and fear all around
Too many tears have been shed
    My heart broken, filled with pain
Our governments crossed the line
    Broke laws again and again
The law of respect is gone
    The law of inclusion lost
The law of love cast aside
    The law of compromise tossed
Political Parties are destroying it all
    We sit and watch hopelessly
As ignorance spreads like fire
    Abusing authority
Our country won't ever be the same
    Division has struck its blow
Too late to turn back the clock
    And act like you did not know
Soon you will see what I say
    And divided we will be
United we will not stand
    Severed in two - maybe three

THE HUMBLE

The humble know how much there is to understand.
Those who understand
know how much more there is to understand.
The proud, those who think they understand,
speak with a boastful and arrogant mouth,
only proving themselves to be fools.

I LOVE YOU

Do I tell you I love you too much
    is it possible that one can do so
Many don't say it enough
    but can you say it too much, I don't know

I do know that when I tell you
    I mean it each and every time
For my love for you now is much greater
    than years past when you were first mine

I hope you don't get tired of hearing
    me tell you that I love you so much
I would rather tell you too often
    than regret I've not told you enough

I love you.

THAT MOMENT

That moment – THAT MOMENT!
I've lived over and over again
these so many years.
Wanting so badly to return
to that one night.
After years of being closest of friends;
having shared all of our dreams, laughter, and tears.
That moment you looked at me
and said so softly, "Kiss me."
As we held each other close,
the embrace was gentle and warm.
Our lips touched and
our tongues danced.
I was not ready for it.
I was not emotionally prepared.
And you were not ready
for how I reacted.
My insecurities poured out
and I clung to you in desperation.
I had loved you all along,
never thinking that you could love me.
But when you opened your heart,
I was just not ready.
Though I so badly wanted to be.
And I lost you forever,
in that moment.

I NEVER HAVE EVER

I see your face everywhere - I hear your voice too
I look and I see your smile - and say I love you
I cannot deny that - I never have known

A love held within my heart - so pure and so true
I can't get you off my mind - nor do I want to
You're all that I've wanted - and even more so

I never have ever known, a love that's so right
I never have ever felt, so free and alive
I never have ever been, so sure in my heart
I never, no, never want, to ever be apart

To hold you close in my arms - is all that I need
To have you here by my side - just to feel you breathe
It's just so amazing - how love came to be

And now as I look - into your gentle brown eyes
So beautiful standing there - in the moonlight
And no, it has never - ever been this good

I never have ever known, a love that's so right
I never have ever felt, so free and alive
I never have ever been, so sure in my heart
I never, no, never want, to ever be apart

DEBT

Debt
is a prison,
I put myself in.
It confines me
behind bars
of regret and
isolation.
It weighs
me down.
Suffocates me.
Squeezes me
until there is nothing
more.
I just want
to be free.

A FAIR WARNING

George Washington gave us fair warning
    in his sobering farewell address
How political parties would harm the nation
    divide us and cause such distress

He warned us how a party faction
    could take power by fear and alarm
Building distrust in one another
    exploiting differences, anger, and harm

Pitting one side against the other
    the north against south, east against west
The poor against the rich, dividing asunder
    turmoil abounding and reckless unrest

"Nobody's right if everybody's wrong"
    a powerful line in a protest song
It rings true more than ever this day
    as we've lost all will to get along

So, here we are divided in this country
    Washington was obviously right
A faction of a party has severed the land
    and darkness now rules over light

George Washington gave us fair warning
    in his sobering farewell address
And we chose not to heed or to listen
    Now divided we stand a chaotic mess

LIVE THE TRUTH

Everyone can justify
what it is
they have convinced themselves
to believe.
But the truth is still
the truth.
In the end
the truth will prevail
and in its wake
will be the carcasses
of those left
to their own lie.
Live the truth.

THE DARK AND THE LIGHT

I have lived with the dark,
all of my life.
Early on, if not for flashes of light,
I would have dove into the darkness.
During those days, I hung by my fingernails
onto every stream of light I could find.
Some days got very dark.
I could feel the earth swallowing me.
But I made it through
and learned to fight.
I kicked at the darkness,
to see streams of light.
Then I knew, that after the dark,
the light would come.
Now the dark visits me
while I bask in the light.
It is there to remind me,
it is waiting.
The light is now much brighter
as my latter years pass.
I am grateful,
I did not give in.
I did not allow
the darkness to win.

REGRETS AND WORRIES

Regrets are past circumstances
    that did not turn out so well
Worries are future circumstances
    will it be okay – you just can't tell

Regrets in the past can't be undone
    the best you can do is learn from them
Worries of the future can't be resolved
    by stressing out and causing mayhem

The past has been and the future will be
    but to stay sane – just deal with today
Think about each choice and make good ones
    regrets will be few – worries go away

So, today is really all there is
    get past the regrets – toss worries aside
Focus on the now and all will be fine
    today is where comfort and peace abide

DEFEATED

If you choose to believe
that you are who you are,
what you are,
and where you are
because of some destiny
that you cannot change
or overcome
then you are defeated.

RESPECT

With pure love comes respect.
Respect never belittles.
Respect never insults.
Respect never degrades.
Respect never sees race.
Respect never points out flaws
of those whom you care for.
Respect is the purest love.

WAKE AND WATCH YOU SLEEP

In the middle of this quiet night
I awake and see you lying there
Your head rests softly on the pillow
The moonlight shows your skin so fair
I feel a warmth so deep inside my heart
I pray you'll never go away

So, I can, always wake and watch you sleep
Next to me

The love I hold for you so deep within
Feels so peaceful down inside
Never held a woman in my arms
So beautiful before my eyes
As I gaze upon you next to me
I hope you'll always be there

So, I can, always wake and watch you sleep
Next to me

WHERE ARE THE MODERATES?

And so, the far right
    think they are so right
When they are so wrong
    in their self-righteous fight

The far left have their faults
    I see them too
But not as many as
    the self-righteous right do

So, where are the moderates
    to help balance our fate
From the far left and the right
    to bring peace for our sake?

For so many years
    we've been fighting this fight
For equality in races,
    genders, and human rights

Why must we go back
    and fight those battles again
Seems we've not progressed any
    in this chaos we're in

So much for the unity
    divided we will fall
So, trash that pledge saying,
    "liberty and justice for all"

I HAVE BEEN A FOOL

I have been a fool
    more than once
And sometimes for love
    an absolute dunce

I was the greatest fool
    on that day when
Our lives crossed
    and I let you in

You reeled me in
    made me believe
That this was it
    just you and me

Then things got real
    the truth came out
You were just having fun
    leading me about

You crushed my heart
    in your vice of lies
And then you were gone
    without a goodbye

MUSIC CAN HEAL A HEART

Music can heal a heart
    but cannot heal the world
For decades we've tried
    with so many words

Though love is the answer
    hate around us still thrives
And in just a short time
    it has multiplied

Music with a message
    still speaks loud and clear
But fewer are listening
    they just don't want to hear

You can't make someone love
    when their mind has been made
Music cannot get past
    a hardened heart of hate

Music is life for so many
    who know its power
But it is not the cure
    for the evil this hour

Don't get me wrong
    I wish it were so
But music can't heal
    the enmity we now know

EARTHQUAKE WITHIN

Anxiety is crushing in on me
Like an earthquake catastrophe
I feel it running through my body
Destroying hopes – creating insecurities
Shaking the core of all I believe
Leaving dust and ruins within my psyche
Anxiety is an earthquake in my spirit and soul
It takes hold of my heart and won't let go
The earthquake will cease and tremors will come
And after all the destruction and damage is done
I pick up the pieces and move on
Rebuilding stronger my emotional foundation

SEARCHING FOR WHY

We've heard about the evil
    That's come into our lives
We didn't see it coming
    They were falling from the skies
The burning fires shot upward
    All came crashing down
We stood in disbelief
    At the terror all around

Searching for why
Searching for what for
Looking to see
Wanting to know more
Searching for why
Searching for the truth
Searching to find
Hope to hold onto

Reading of the thousands dead
    A tear comes to my eye
For the many who have lost
    Brothers, sisters, husbands, wives
Will the fighting ever end
    Will it ever be done
Will there ever be peace
    From hate and bombs and guns

I'm thinking of the children
    Who have lost their whole lives
Over selfish cold ambitions
    Oh, so many bled and died
It was just another day
    Just another school year
The battle turned it all
    Into floods of bitter tears

Searching for why
Searching for what for
Looking to see
Wanting to know more
Searching for why
Searching for the truth
Searching to find
Hope to hold onto

LONG TO HAVE YOU HERE

The days they've turned to weeks then turned to months
Since I last held you so close
That I felt your heartbeat, saw your gentle eyes
Like the petals of a rose

How my heart calls out at night, as I lay down
Softly whisper your name
How I ache to taste your lips and feel your skin
Walk with you out in the rain

I long to have you here
So long to have you here - With me

I sit alone, just staring at the walls
As my mind remembers when
I held you tight, that very first night
As we felt the evening's wind

Yes, it seems so cruel to love so much
When you're miles away from me
Cause beside you, with you in my arms
Is where I want to be

I long to have you here
So long to have you here - With me

WHY?

Why do you
lie to yourself?

I REMEMBER EVERY MOMENT

Sometimes I wonder where you are
    what you are doing - if you are okay
Forty-plus years have passed us by
    I hope life's been good - along the way

You were a friend so dear to me
    so wise and thoughtful - in choices you made
I was reckless in making mine
    depression took hold - was the price I paid

I remember every moment
    that we shared - those so many years ago
We would get in the car and drive
    to listen to music - or catch a show

They are times that I hold closely
    every laugh, tear - and mem'ry shared
Is forever a treasured part
    of my past life – when you were always there

I USED TO WRITE SONGS

I used to write songs
    but they never sold
They weren't good enough
    or so I was told

Maybe it was my voice
    or my lack of style
Maybe it was the music
    or my playing all the while

For whatever reason
    they never took off
And so my dreams
    Forever were lost

With any art form
    it is that way
You do your best
    then hope and pray

Now I just write
    for better or worse
For richer or poorer
    favored or cursed

All I can hope for
    all I wish to see
Is a broken heart healed
    by my words that they read

STRUGGLES WITHIN THIS SKIN

People all around me, walk right on by
Lost in their lonely world, of self-driven pride
Stuck in their troubles, buried in pain
No sight of relief, no hope to be gained

We've lost sight of goodness, and the love deep within
These are the struggles within this skin

There are wars all over, blood running so deep
The children are dying, their mothers weep
Children killing children, in our backyards
Hate is so bitter when the heart is so hard

Where's all this heading – when will it end
These are the struggles within this skin

Drugs flow so freely, into their veins
Hiding their heart from the hurt and the pain
Got to stand up now, speak loud and clear
Going to shout it all over 'til everyone hears

Got to stand up and shout it, again and again
These are the struggles within this skin

Time to put aside hate, time to put aside self
Time to put aside greed and help someone else
Time to stop in our tracks, and look deep inside
Time to stop all the foolishness, got to stop all the lies

Got to get past the ignorance, and learn love again
To fight all these struggles within this skin

WE HAVE NOTHING

We have nothing.
We possess nothing.
We own nothing.
We accumulate nothing.
Everything is given to us
to cherish and care for.
We were given the earth,
and we are destroying it.
And yet we are so proud.

WASTE AND WANT

If all who have
would stop wasting.
Then the many who want,
would have.

JUSTICE AND INJUSTICE

Justice and injustice
    Words void of truth
In this world in which we live
Perverted by perversions
    From minds of men
Who only take and never give

The poor become poorer
    The rich want more
Moderation is long gone
Alone and lonely
    Their cries are heard
But little is ever done

One race over all races
    Is what they want
The ideal of supremacy
Oppress the oppressed
    Back to the wall
Where life is never easy

Hope for the hopeless
    Is all we ask
Just to listen to their plea
Dreams left for dreamers
    Is that so bad
To have true equality

WE ARE SO PROUD

We are so proud
    of all the progress
In technology we've made
    in becoming the best
How it benefits us
    in extending our lives
Making us more beautiful
    as perfection we strive
It is so pleasant
    to be in the know
Of all things around us
    such wonder to behold
Yes, such progress we've made
    for all the world to see
So powerfully influential
    so many – so happy
We have all that we need
    in our world as of late
Yet we still have no answer
    for our divisions and hate

YOU COLOR MY WORLD

With colors bright and true
With reds and brilliant blues
With all your love within
You color my world

You opened up my heart
Lit my deepest dark
And when you smile at me
You color my world

The sun rises to shine
And light the morning sky
It can't compare with how
You color my world

No rainbow that has shone
No painters ever known
The many ways I see
You color my world

The flowers in the spring
Do not begin to bring
The life you give to me
You color my world

So, walk here by my side
Spend the rest of our lives
And from now until then
You'll color my world

And from now until then
You'll color my world

THE TWO OF US

The two of us finding each other
    much later in our lives
Has been so good in many ways
    And in love a great surprise

Neither of us saw it coming
    unexpected to say the least
But here we are so happy in love
    content in our sanctum of peace

It's true that the world is changing
    around us each and every day
We are fortunate to have seen its best
    it's sad watching it rot and decay

But in our little home where we live
    and love to the fullest we can
We hope that the chaos will cease
    and we return to order again

Until then we hold each other closely
    laugh, learn, and love all the while
And look for the beauty around us
    and cherish each moment and smile

TRUE HEARING

You cannot see unless you open your eyes.
You cannot speak unless you open your mouth.
You cannot touch unless you reach out your hand.
But though sounds may enter your ears,
you cannot truly hear if you do not open your heart,
open your mind,
and receive it in your soul.

THE POWER OF SELFLESSNESS

Overcome by indulgent selfishness,
we have become too lazy to exert the selfless strength
it would require to produce equality and peace.
Hate and war take lives.
Peace takes selfless lives.

SO IT GOES

"So, it goes"
    Kurt Vonnegut wrote
In *Slaughterhouse-Five*
    it is a quote
To a fond farewell
    or a new beginning
So, it is what life is
    at the start or its ending
"So, it goes"
    and it does
We start and end
    what it was
Death has its say
    and so does life
Throughout the struggles
    toil and strife
"So, it goes"
    so, it is
So, we go on
    for now we live

"So, it goes"

GO AHEAD

Go ahead and live
   in your ignorance of bliss
Accept all the lies
   from the government abyss

Go ahead and wear
   your rose-colored glasses
As they dismantle democracy
   and burn it to ashes

Go ahead and support
   the elephant in the room
As they divide this country
   and send it to its doom

Go ahead and be proud
   of all the hate they have spread
As they spew propaganda
   igniting chaos and dread

Go ahead and laugh
   at all their degrading jokes
About migrants and races
   and less fortunate folks

Go ahead and worship
   the idol you've made
As your freedoms are stripped
   and our democracy fades

THAT GUY

I was that guy in high school.
You know the one.
In all my yearbooks
they would write,
"To a sweet guy."
If I got lucky,
"To a cute guy."
Never "hot."
Never "handsome."
Never "cool."
Never "awesome."
Just "sweet" and "cute."
Like a favorite stuffed animal
or maybe a pet.
That's okay.
I'm still here.

LOVED ONES LOST

This one's for the moms
    this one's for the dads
This one's for the brothers and sisters
And the memories long past
This one's for the children
    the husbands and the wives
This one's for the many friends
Whose broken hearts have cried

For the many who have gone before
    That have paid the ultimate cost
You will never be forgotten
    We mourn our loved ones lost

This one's for our country
    whose heartaches and cries
Are looking for some hope and truth
In the midst of all the lies
This one's for the government
    with hope that they will seek
Wisdom and compassion
So, the bloodshed will cease

For the many who have gone before
    That have paid the ultimate cost
You will never be forgotten
    We mourn our loved ones lost

From the past until the present
To the future ahead
Your memory we will honor
Our brave hearted dead

For they stood strong in battle
    Paid the ultimate cost
No, they will never be forgotten
    We mourn our loved ones lost

POSITIVITY IS AN ILLUSION

Positivity is an illusion
A toxic delusion
Destructive by nature
In its mindset solution

It's a lost cause
In this lost world
That's not being negative,
That's being objective

IT IS NOT JUST LOVE

It is not just love
    that makes who we are
That has mended the wounds
    and healed all the scars
For between us there is
    a respect that we share
It runs deep in our lives
    showing in how we care
I know I have never
    felt so at home
As when we're together
    the two of us alone
Love is not strong enough
    a word to describe
All that you are to me
    and how it's so right
You have brightened my darkness
    you have colored my world
Now we're bound in a love
    so rich, full, and pure

THEN AND NOW

The decade of the 1960's.
Many died for what they believed.
Not just on foreign soil,
but here on our own soil.
They faced jeering, spitting,
hatred, and abuse.
They were beaten and hanged.
They were burned. They were martyrs.
For what?
Their belief – that all people
are created equal.
Just as our forefathers said.

The 1960's songs said all the right things.
Peace, love, and harmony.
Love was the message to all.
They stood shoulder to shoulder,
defiant against the machine.
Four were senselessly killed in Ohio.
That did not stop the fight.
They kept marching hand in hand.
Why?
Their belief – that all people
are created equal.
Just as our forefathers said.

So many words were spoken
So many good intentions of the heart.
So many that bled and died.
So many gave all they had.
So many marched loud and proud.
So many shouted for their rights.
So many in that decade.
So many, too many, died fighting.
Now what in 2025?
Are all people created equal?
To the white privileged, racists, and fascists-
obviously not.

FOR A MOMENT

For a moment
We were there
At that place
Two hearts share

The touching of hands
The pleasure of smiles
The instance of life
Where emotions run wild

The look in the eyes
The caress of the skin
The whisper of hope
Where attraction begins

For a moment
We were there
A heart check
Made aware

The moment was bliss
Two heartbeats so close
It was only a moment
Then we had to let it go

OPEN YOUR EYES

Look. LOOK!
Open your eyes
and see.
If you can
that is.
Many are blind
by choice.
Refusing to see
the truth in front of them.
Why?
A hard heart?
Stubbornness?
Pride and arrogance?
Ignorance?
Why?
Maybe, just maybe
they might see
what they do not want to see.
That they have
played the fool.
Open your eyes
and see the lie.

PERSPECTIVE

All of us die.
Some already have.
Some of us will die sooner than others.
But eventually, we will all die.

It is sad that we only have absolute clarity
at that moment when we are taking our last breath.
Why is it that we have to wait until that moment
to understand what is really important?
Why is it that we cannot let go of things
that are so irrelevant in this life
and embrace instead the things
that are truly important?
Why have we allowed material indulgences
to oppress us into financial bondage
when in that last moment,
none of it will save us.

At that moment, all things become clear.
There is only one thing that anyone wants
as they take their final breath:
to be able to take one more breath.

Breathe deeply and ask yourself,
"Is what I'm doing really all that important?
Is what I am struggling for really worth it?
How much will any of this mean to me
as I take my last breath?"

MATTERS OF THE HEART

Four hours.
Anxiety gripped my world.
I was healthy.
For a couple of weeks,
a recurring dull pain
around my left chest.
Pulled muscle?
Gas pain?
It came and went.
Then last night, the pain
followed by a sharp pain
that travelled to my left armpit.
Apprehension.
Emergency Room.
EKG. Chest X-Ray.
Blood work.
At least two hours passed.
More blood work.
Then the prognosis.
My heart was fine.
No signs of problems.
Maybe a pulled muscle?
Follow up with doctor.
Peace.
Gratefulness.
Home.
Sleep easy.

YOUR VOICE

Your voice slices through the air
    cuts into my heart
Words mingle with my memories
    ripping them apart

Raising emotions and heartache
    each wistful melody
Every lingering note played
    rings pure and tenderly

My life revealed with ethereal tones
    my secrets all exposed
With every floating syllable
    my painful past composed

As I attentively listen
    lost in this poignant art
It pierces insecurities
    as a well thrown dart

While "Various Storms and Saints"
    march around my head
The bleeding has now stopped
    as I lie upon my bed

And though I do not know you
    our paths have never crossed
I know the pain, the hurtful cries
    the regrets of moments lost

But soothing is your voice I hear
    so, calming to my soul
I know I'll be okay and soon
    will continue on life's stroll

WANT TO LET YOU KNOW

I had held you close in my thoughts so many years
I never thought I'd see your eyes again
There you sat before me looking as you did back then
I stumbled at the words inside my head

It's funny how some words just seem so hard
You want to say them right, so they're not taken wrong
So, I'll just sit and write them from this chair
Cause I just want to tell you, I just want to let you know – I care

In this present situation that I see you going through
I wish that I could say what's on my mind
Some things are best unspoken and just written from the heart
Cause the heart knows more than words in hurting times

Now as I rest my pen and send this off to you
I find myself in search of words to say
Just how I think about you and the warmth it brings to me
And how your smile is in my heart to stay

It's funny how some words just seem so hard
You want to say them right, so they're not taken wrong
So, I'll just sit and write them from this chair
Cause I just want to tell you, I just want to let you know – I care

TWO WORDS

Two words – what a curse
   that they should even exist
That they could cause such pain
   in a moment of bliss

Two words – that when spoken
   conjure memories and regrets
Though you so badly wish you could
   you can never forget

Two words – then so much pain
   brings the past back to haunt you
And you try to block it out
   push it aside and break on through

Two words – what a curse
   that they should even exist-

If only...

ONE MOMENT YOU ARE WITH US

One moment you are with us
   and the next you are not
One moment you are remembered
   and in another you're forgot
It will come to us, that moment
   we will all have in this life
One moment we are living
   in the next we simply die
It is how we all will end one day
   that moment will surely come
Our last breath we will slowly breathe
   and then suddenly we are gone
It may happen at an early age
   or allow us to grow old
But that moment will come for all of us
   all our warmth will turn to cold
Then buried will our body be
   lowered into the ground
Where all our senses will come to cease
   silence will be the only sound

THE SOUND OF AUTHORITARIAN FASCISM

Are you listening?
Do you see what is happening?
It crumbles so easily,
what once was so brave and free.
So quickly it slips away,
when we believed it would always stay.
It crumbles before our eyes.
Laid bare by deceit and lies.
The beauty of our democracy,
laid waste by pride and the racist disease.
The free world is being brought low.
The light being snuffed out by fascists grows.
Are you listening?
Do you see what is happening?
My heart breaks,
for all our sakes.
As democracy is taken down,
and replaced by an oppressive sound.
The sound of authoritarian fascism.

JOY AND SORROW

Joy and sorrow are our two greatest emotions.
We should be grateful for both.
Joy allows us to see all the blessings.
Sorrow allows us to gain understanding.

DON'T WALK AWAY

Come-Love in the morning
Come-Love in the noon time
Come-Love in the evening
Come-Love with me now

Come-Take my hand softly
Come-Walk with me slowly
Come-Spend some time with me
Come-Love with me now

Take from me all that I give
Love with me till the day ends
Look into my eyes and see
Come love with me

Come-Look at me closely
Come-see my heart open
Come-I love you so wholly
Come-Love with me now

Come-I cannot endure this
Come-Take me as you wish
Come-I only want you please
Come-Love with me now

Turn to me say it's okay
Come to me in my arms stay
Look to me know this today
I'm here to stay
So don't walk away

WHISPERING LOVES LULLABY

Had it been a different day another moment
We might have passed each other by
Circumstance and fate aligned our paths to cross here
On this quiet summer night

We sit as silence covers all of the room
Where we've come to spend some time
And in the quiet, I can hear your heartbeat softly
You slip your hand gently in mine

As I look at you, your eyes brightly shine
From the candlelight nearby
My heart is fixed upon, a voice so deep inside
Whispering loves lullaby

The night is young and minutes turn to hours
As we laugh and talk of life
It's not what's been but what is now that really matters
That makes this moment feel so right

When I start to leave, we hold each other closely
With a soft and knowing smile
Looking forward to the promise of tomorrow
And what could be in our new lives

As I look at you, your eyes brightly shine
From the candlelight nearby
My heart is fixed upon, a voice so deep inside
Whispering loves lullaby

FAITH AND LOVE

GOD IS

God is.
God is not
what men want God to be.
For God is not
a bull-headed he.
Nor is God
a much wiser she.
For God is They,
The Holy Trinity,
yet one Holy Deity.
The Creator, Beloved, and Presence
three spirit entities.
Yes, separate spirits,
in perfect harmony,
as They have been
all eternity.
For God is spirit,
not of flesh, you see.
God is much more
than you or me.
God is and reigns,
in all Their majesty.
God is everything,
and is all I need.
God is,
is what I believe.

THE SIGNS ARE ALL THERE

"Ask, and it will be given to you; search, and you will find; knock, and the door will be opened for you. For everyone who asks receives, and everyone who searches finds, and for everyone who knocks, the door will be opened." [Jesus said to His followers]
Matthew 7:7-8

Knock and You will open
   seek and we will find
That no matter how dark
   Your light of love shines

Your light might seem dim
   these days that we live
But it is still bright
   as the hope that it gives

You warned us these days
   would come near the end
And when it seems too much
   Your peace you will send

We must stay awake
   we must stay aware
Keep our eyes open
   the signs are all there

A PERSONAL GOD

God is a personal God.
God loves each of us.
God has no favor of gender or race.
God deals with each of us individually.
Yes, corporately we are the spiritual church.
Yes, corporately we are the bride of Jesus Christ.
But at the end of the ages, we will be judged individually
by the motives of our hearts.
Too many make their church building their God.
Too many make their denomination their God.
Too many make their doctrines their God.
And they will be judged accordingly -
for the harm they have caused -
individually.

THE ETERNAL DEBATE

They say that God does not exist
I say that I know that God is
They say this started with a big bang
I say that God created the big bang
They say that we came through evolution
I say show me the missing links
They say humankind created God
I say God created humankind
They say if God is love why is there suffering
I say we are responsible for the suffering
They say science says there is no God
I say science cannot prove there is not a God
They say there is no afterlife
I say how do you know?
They say, "There is intelligent life out there somewhere."
I say, "I agree with that."
They say, "What do you mean?"
I say, "God is intelligent."

GOD KNEW

God knew in Lucifer
   evil would come
Lucifer would grow proud
   and rebellion begun

God knew that hate
   would be born
And the devil would rise
   to divide and scorn

God knew and yet
   Satan came to be
God's plan was set
   for all eternity

LORD, GIVE ME

Lord, give me
   the strength within
To walk away
   from sin

Make my heart
   desire to do right
And never do wrong
   in Your sight

Fill me with
   Your Spirit of truth
That in all things
   I will please You

Help me to
   ever be aware
To love all people
   to always care

So, when I stand
   before Your throne
You'll speak these words,
   "Welcome home."

WHO OH GOD IS LIKE YOU

Who oh God is like You
None can ever say
Your glory and Your splendor
Are revealed to us each day

Your majesty and power
Are seen in creation
Your grace and forgiveness
Are here for everyone

GOD IS SO MUCH MORE

God is so much more
    than we can understand
Though we think we are able
    there's no way that we can

God is vaster by far
    in wisdom beyond ours
We cannot comprehend
    God's limitless powers

If we could – I think
    that's rather odd
That a mere human being
    could truly understand God

THE FRUIT OF THE SPIRIT

Love, the greatest gift of all
    to receive or to give in this life
Joy does not have to be outwardly shown
    but can be salve, to sooth pain and strife
Peace comes, when we release all worries
    to a God who cares and loves us so
Patience is a virtue, that's so needed today
    in planting a seed and watching it grow
Kindness can tear down, walls that hatred builds
    that make life so hard to cope
Goodness will heal; the wounds so deep
    when there seems no glimmer of hope
Gentleness can break, the hardest of hearts
    where there's anger, restore peace
Faithfulness will provide, a bond of trust
    when someone is ill at ease
Self-control is the discipline, to do right
    when you might get by with wrong
The fruit of the Spirit, is what we need
    in this life to restore hope and stay strong

ON THE DAY WE STAND TO TAKE ACCOUNT

There is no gender or race in the eyes of God
   there is only the soul within
The soul is either righteous or unrighteous
   it is either pure or full of sin

That is it and that is all
   that comes out of this life
For God sees only what your soul has done
   either it was wrong or it was right

You may say that there is always grey
   all things cannot be just black or white
But you are wrong, for in God's eyes
   all truth stands out above the lies

Truth is all that will stand that day
   all the inner motives will be exposed
Lies and deception will not stand
   God's Righteousness will not allow it so

No gender or race will matter then
   nor white privilege or royal birth
On the day we stand to take account
   of the life we lived upon this earth

BELIEVING VERSUS FAITH

Believing in God
and having faith in God
are two different things.
To say you believe
in God
is merely accepting what is.
But having faith
in God
is to know
without question,
without doubt,
without wavering,
that you know -
with all certainty,
with all surety,
with all confidence,
God is.

THE LOVE OF MONEY

One of the most misquoted verses of the Scriptures is,
"Money is the root of all evil".
It actually states,
"For the LOVE of money is A root of ALL KINDS of evil."
The lust, the desire to have, the greed, the coveting of money
which is selfish ambition; is A root of ALL KINDS of evil;
be it hatred, bitterness, envy, murder, anger, and the like.
Know the Scriptures, before misquoting the Scriptures.

THE ANTICHRIST AND THE FALSE PROPHET

The spirit of the antichrist
   spoken of in First John
Is the spirit that says Jesus
   could not possibly be God's Son
It denies that Jesus Christ
   is one in the Deity
And surely there's no truth
   in the blessed Trinity
The antichrist spirit says
   that Jesus was just a man
He might have been a prophet
   but nothing more you understand
This is how the spirit of the antichrist
   tries to confuse and deceive
It wants to contradict
   what Jesus taught us to believe
The spirit of the false prophet
   is itself a different sort
It will take a single verse
   twist the meaning and distort
As Jesus rebuked those in Pergamum
   for accepting Nicolaitan lies
Having twisted His teachings of truth
   and promoting undisciplined lives
Jesus also rebuked Thyatira
   for following lies of Jezebel
Approving fornication in a holy life
   perverting the Scriptures as well

The spirits of the antichrist
    and false prophet thrive today
Within the churches across our land
    lies are told and demon's prey
Beware the spirit of the antichrist
    beware the false prophet too
Pray that the Spirit of our loving God
    helps you discern the lies from the truth

NAME OF ALL NAMES

How many times have I sat alone
    Feeling no peace
I wrestle with thoughts that I know are wrong
    And I become weak
I cry out to you, Lord
And you come to me
You show me your Word
So, my eyes can see
The name of all names
Has stood faithfully

Provider, Protector, the God of Peace
    Healer and the Righteous One
Sanctifier and the God who's there
    Shepherd for all who will come
You are the God called the Great I Am
    All that you ever proclaim
You sit on Your throne lifted up so high
    Bearing the name of all names
Jehovah God

I look all around me and see the hurt
    So many I know
Are caught in the trap of the devil's lie
    And they can't let go
But You see them all, Lord
And Your heart does break
Oh, we must go tell them
That You are the way
The name of all names
Still loves them today

Provider, Protector, the God of Peace
    Healer and the Righteous One
Sanctifier and the God who's there
    Shepherd for all who will come
You are the God called the Great I Am
    All that you ever proclaim
You sit on Your throne lifted up so high
    Bearing the name of all names
Jehovah God

SO SHALL IT BE

As Your Word Says,
so shall it be.
Your will
be done on this earth.
Your plan
will come to pass.
Your prophecies
will be fulfilled.
This earth
and creation will be no more.
All that will be left
will be the judgment.
The books will be open.
The Book of Life will be open.
And we all will be
judged according
to what we have done
in Your eyes.
The righteous will proceed
into eternal peace in Your presence.
The unrighteous will proceed
into eternal damnation and torment.
As Your Word says,
so shall it be.

INFECTED SORES

Holding on to what is here
    is missing out on so much
Material gain and possessions
    are meaningless and shallow
They are band-aids on infected sores
    that will never heal
Satisfaction for a brief moment
    then the emptiness returns
A life full of purpose
    with contentment and peace
Is when you are truly living
    when you are truly alive

SOMETIMES MY FAITH

Sometimes my faith
  is not that strong
I question myself
  and what's going on

My spirit is willing
  but my flesh is weak
I close my eyes
  Your Grace I seek

These days it's hard
  such chaos and pain
I search through Your Word
  to find truth again

You always come through
  and I am able to see
And Your Presence of comfort
  comes rest upon me

I know You are God
  and You wish us to grow
The times we grow weak
  Grace won't let us go

OUR GOD AND OUR LORD

We've searched 'cross the oceans
   Sailed many a sea
Looked into the heavens
To find why we live
   What we can be
With questions abounding
   We seek just to find
What's right before our eyes
If we will just look
   And turn from the lie

Our God and our Lord
The Maker and Savior of the world

Death surrounds us from every side
   Evil dances in the light
The world spirals downward
Lost in its sin
   Blind in the night
Answers never will be found
   By wisdom of man
But only in Jesus
Will truth come to be
   And healing of our land

Our God and our Lord
The Maker and Savior of the world

PRO-LOVE

What is Pro-Choice?
What is Pro-Life?
But more man-made doctrine
From the left and the right

Jesus taught us to Love
To do what is good
To love from our hearts
Is clearly understood

Pro-Choice or Pro-Life?
But I have one greater
Pro-Love is my creed
There is none any better

Pro-Love does what's right
No matter the case
To help the hurting
In whatever they face

Pro-Love is God's love
Flowing through Their own
To heal the pain
And the damage done

SOMETIMES IN OUR LIVES

Sometimes in our lives, something comes our way
That we'd like to have, that we'd like to stay
But what we want and what we need
Is not always the same and so we plead
Why can't You just let me have, this one little thing
You know all the happiness to me it would bring

And so, you may ponder and think of a way
That you may hold onto it and feel it's okay
But deep down inside, you know it's wrong
And so, you may hurt, but you've got to be strong
Don't let it get you down, so far down the road
That you lose all sight of truth and it becomes a heavy load

Sometimes in our lives, we have to let go
Of all the things, deep down that we know
Have come in between, what we have to do
And though it hurts, God pulls us through
But it always turns out to be, what we needed from the start
Not just to obey, we must mean it from the heart

So, look to the one, who gave it all
Without any questions, He obeyed His call
And if you still feel, that it's just not fair
You better look twice, at that heart you wear
For if you cannot give up and let it all go
Then there's no use in trying -
to understand what you think you know

JESUS MY LORD

Jesus my Lord
Your name so holy and so rightfully adored
Jesus my Lord
I want to praise Your name from distant shore to shore

Jesus my Lord
Your guiding light so present and forever more
Jesus my Lord
Your grace abounding and Your love so very sure

MERCY

I thank God
for all of the times
things did not happen
that could have.
All those times
that God's mercy
stopped things
from going too far.
I thank God
for mercy.

EVIL IS NOT

Evil is not
    the opposite of good
For those with understanding
    this is understood
Holy is the true
    opposite of evil
For Holy is our God
    and evil is the devil
The opposite of good
    is simply being bad
Good is what we hope for
    bad just makes us sad
Empathy has an opposite
    apathy is its name
But empathy without action
    is apathy just the same
Our God being Holy
    wishes us to be good
Having empathy for our neighbors
    and acting as we should
And when evil rises
    we must stand and fight
With our Holy God before us
    evil has no might
Holiness, goodness, and empathy
    gifts given from above
For in every one of these
    is the presence of God's love

MORE OF YOUR LOVE

Lord, let me show them more of Your mercy
Lord, let me see what Your truth's made of
Lord, let me be more willing to follow
That, Lord, I may show them more of Your love

Lord now I see the lie that I've lived
I see through the veil of deceit
I come to You and ask that You give
Me a heart that seeks Yours restlessly

Soften my heart, search deep within
Show me my darkest desires
Cleanse me with truth, purge out the sin
Consume my lust with Your Holy fire

Lord, let me show them more of Your mercy
Lord, let me see what Your truth's made of
Lord, let me be more willing to follow
That, Lord, I may show them more of Your love

JESUS INSTRUCTED US

Jesus did not instruct us
to build million-dollar edifices.
Jesus instructed us to
edify people – all people.
To strengthen and build them up
in spirit – for His glory – not ours.
Jesus instructed us to be poor in spirit –
humble – recognizing His Sovereignty.
Jesus instructed us to comfort those who mourn –
to be compassionate and caring.
Jesus instructed us to be meek –
recognizing that He detests pride.
Jesus instructed us to hunger and thirst
for righteousness – always seeking to do right.
Jesus instructed us to be merciful –
always acknowledging the mercy He has shown us.
Jesus instructed us to be pure in heart –
realizing that He does not tolerate lies and deception.
Jesus instructed us to always seek peace
over confrontation, hatred, and war.
Jesus instructed us that we would be persecuted
for abiding in His truth.
Jesus never instructed us to hate our enemies,
He instructed us to love them.
Jesus left us with explicit instructions
to live by...what's not to understand?

LORD OF MERCY

Lord of mercy
    Lord so Holy
Lord so full of grace
I adore you
    Come before you
And I seek Your face

Let Your kingdom come
Let Your will be done

PROSPERITY AND JUDGMENT

YOU CANNOT CLAIM the prosperity verses
of the Scriptures and discard the verses on judgment.
To do so is hypocrisy.

Yes, Jesus proclaimed love, joy, peace, patience,
kindness, goodness, gentleness, faithfulness,
self-control, and many other very positive
characteristics of a believer's heart.

But Jesus also proclaimed
that prior to the end of the ages
there would be great anxiety,
debauchery, false prophets,
wars and rumors of wars,
nations rising against nations,
famines, pestilences, earthquakes,
persecution of believers,
the love of many growing cold,
parents betraying children,
children betraying parents,
siblings betraying siblings.

The first Beast and second Beast already exist.
The image of the Beast has been created.
A cashless society is just around the corner
and will usher in the mark of the beast.
The modern Babylon of the United States
will fall and will be taken over by its enemies.
Jerusalem will be surrounded by its enemies
and the desolation will occur.
There will be great suffering
as has never been seen since the beginning of time,
and there will be cosmic displays of stress and destruction.

God is a just God whose mercy endures forever
for those who are righteous.
We cannot discard these truths.
The end of the ages is unfolding before us.
Stay awake. Stay aware.

THE EARTH EMBRACES THE DEAD

The earth embraces the dead.
Every human being
that has walked upon this earth
is still among us
in one form or another.
Whether the earth
has swallowed up the blood
that flowed from their being
or their body has rotted
into the depths of the ground,
every single person
that has walked on this earth
is a part of it.
Whether they died
from being murdered,
a war,
an accident,
a sickness,
or natural causes,
they are all here.
The earth embraces them
and in its own way,
the earth mourns for them
and cries out to its creator.

SPIRITUAL DEATH

Bitterness, retaliation, and vengeance
from an unforgiving heart is like cancer.
It spreads rapidly
until it consumes the whole body,
causing spiritual death.
Learn to forgive.
Forgive and you will be forgiven.

THIS THANKSGIVING DAY

When we were young, we'd always hear the church bells ring
    Every Sunday morning
Our Mom and Dad would get us out of bed
    Say a prayer before we're fed
We would go to church and listen to the Word
    Fellowship with all our friends
We'd come home and Mom would cook our food
    Dad would give thanks - as we should
We always felt we'd never leave or go astray
    We always felt it'd be that way
I often wonder what our lives would be like now
    Without a Mom and Dad who cared

Lord, we thank You
For the Son You gave who died for all our sins
For without Him we could never enter in
The gates of Heaven
And we thank You
For the life and love You've given us today
And to You we praise on this Thanksgiving Day
This our family, we thank You

But now we're older and we live away from home
    Mom and Dad are left alone
Sometimes when I'm home I'll hear my mother pray
    God keep them in Your Holy way
Keep them safe and give them strength to carry on
    For they are weak but You are strong
Now Lord I have a special prayer of my own
    That when You come, we'll have a home
All of us and let not one be left behind
    Give us strength to let Your light shine
And as we leave to go our separate ways again
    We'd like to say just one more time

Lord, we thank You
For the Son You gave who died for all our sins
For without Him we could never enter in
The gates of Heaven
And we thank You
For the life and love You've given us today
And to You we praise on this Thanksgiving Day
This our family, we thank You

PILATE ASKED JESUS

Pilate asked Jesus, "What is truth?"
Jesus could have answered.
But it would not have mattered.
Do you see that?
Do you understand that?

MERCY AND GRACE

To you, oh God,
    I give you thanks
For all Your mercy
    and most abundant grace

For more than once
    You found me lost
Broken and humbled
    at such a cost

But you could see
    me now back then
You knew I'd get here
    through all the sin

To where I am
    now peace abides
I hold Your hand
    as days pass by

I see so clear
    all You have done
To make me into
    what I've become

SCIENCE SAYS AND I BELIEVE

Science says and I believe,
the earth was formed
four billion years ago.
Let's see,
is that not eternity?

Science says and I believe,
theories abound, at least three
Steady, Eternal, and a Bang.
But theory
is not fact once again.

Science says and I believe,
humans came from the earth
from the dirt under our feet.
Humans from dirt?
Yes, I can believe.

Science says and I believe,
we are killing the earth
due to human greed.
Bad humans
who refuse to believe.

Science says and I believe,
that there is intelligent life
out there somewhere.
So astronomical!
So, I ask, just where?

Science says and I believe,
this other life exists
though it can't be seen.
That so?
You need faith to believe in science?

So, science believes in extra-terrestrial beings.
This too I believe.
God is so much more of an intelligent being than we are.
Maybe God is what science is looking for?
By faith I believe.

EACH DAY I LIVE

Each day I live
   each moment I breathe
Brings me closer to
   my eternity
Where once eternity
   seemed so far away
It is now much closer
   in my latter days
This too means
   death is closer
I know this well
   life ends for sure
I breathe each breath
   thankful for the last
And hopeful for another
   as my hours pass
Each day I live
   each moment I breathe
Inches me closer to
   my eternity

THERE IS HOPE IN GOD

There is hope in God
    but no one else
Not your family or friends
    not even yourself

Hope springs eternal
    in God our Creator
For in God is truth
    there's no love that's greater

My hope rests in God
    this I do know
God won't let me down
    God won't let me go

As long as I do
    what is right and good
I can hope in God
    this is understood

There is hope in God
    I know it's true
And God's peace abides
    when God's hope is in you

I BELIEVE IN DEI [Diversity, Equity, and Inclusion]

I believe in DEI
    because I believe in Jesus Christ
I believe in all His teachings
    To do what's just and right

Jesus taught there's no one righteous
    we all have faults within
He taught we are all equal
    and everyone has sin

He taught us to educate
    all people of His love
To have compassion and be wise
    and as harmless as a dove

He taught us to reach out
    to all hurting, blind, and lame
Providing them with comfort
    while teaching them the same

I believe in DEI
    because I believe in Jesus Christ
All that He taught and stood for
    all the reasons He came and died

THE GOOD SAMARITAN

The "Good Samaritan" -
in the parable Jesus shared -
was good because he helped
someone that hated him.
It's easy to help
those who love us.
It takes the love of Jesus,
an amazing selfless love,
to help those who hate us.

LORD, I PRAISE YOU

Lord, I praise You, praise You Lord
    Glory to Your name
Your arm extended down near hell
    And touched my heart again
I was so tired of falling down
    I reached and took Your hand
Before I crawled on bended knees
    Now in Your Word I stand

Lord, I praise You, praise You Lord
    Forever shall I pray
My mind will never think vile thoughts
    You'll tell me what to say
If ever I may fall away
    Your mercy shall endure
And for all my unrighteousness
    Your stripes my only cure

Lord, I praise You, praise You Lord
    Your Spirit I've received
It teaches me the way to live
    And helps my eyes to see
The Word and understand the things
    That blinded men cannot
Then nurtures it deep in my heart
    This vessel You have wrought

Lord, I praise You, praise You Lord
    You've truly set me free
You've given me peace of mind
    To know what I believe
I pray that I may never feel
    That You have turned away
For I alone make my choice on
    If I leave or stay

Lord, I praise You, praise You Lord
For You are worthy of praise

IRONY

Talk about irony.
We say,
such a cruel God
to destroy this earth.
To make this life
come to an end.
Yet look at us,
we're killing
the earth.
A slow death
by suffocation.
Science has
warned us
but we refuse
to listen.
The earth is going to end,
if not by God – surely by men.
So it goes.

MY PAST IS MY PAST

My past is my past
    and not my present
Today is today
    in this I'm content

God not only forgives
    but forgets our sin too
Making only today
    all that we need to do

In confessing our sins
    with a sincere heart
God forgives and forgets
    giving us a new start

So, our past is our past
    just focus on today
And doing what is right
    each and every way

MOTIVES AND INTENTIONS

The motives of your heart
    true intentions – reasons why
Is the truth that God sees
    behind all your pompous lies

Though you can deceive others
    and even yourself too
God knows all the whys and intentions
    that are deep inside of you

Don't think that you will get away
    God sees the lie you live
Behind your phony persona
    the truth behind your motives

Deception is the life you've lived
    but when you stand on judgment day
It will all come out in your nakedness
    exposed and on full display

MODERATION AND DISCIPLINE

Moderation is the power
of being driven by God's wisdom.
Discipline is doing right
when the flesh desires to do wrong.
Moderation and discipline
will bring more success in life,
than foolish behavior
and undisciplined zeal.

YOUR WILL BE DONE

"Your will be done"
Is the hardest one
When all we want for ourselves
Is what we want for our self
"Your will be done"
Is the hardest one
To have faith in

GOD'S JUSTICE

God's justice is pure,
    perfect, and true
Righteous and holy
    in Heaven's view

Justice on earth
    has been so skewed
It's not justice at all
    no, not even true

But, with God above
    judgment will come
Justice will rule
    for each and everyone

BABYLON IS FALLING

God remembered great Babylon and gave her the wine cup of the fury of His wrath.
Revelation 16:19b

For God has put it into their hearts to carry out his purpose by agreeing to give their kingdom (Babylon) to the beast, until the words of God will be fulfilled.
Revelation 17:17

Babylon is falling
    God sees it all
The prophecy was proclaimed
    God made that call

There is nothing that happens
    that God does not know
For They have ordained it
    and it will be so

No need to fear chaos
    for the Scriptures said it would be
Just rest in the peace that God gives
    with our eyes open to see

The hand of God is working
    for those who don't see it's a shame
For not choosing to believe is their fault
    they have only themselves to blame

Babylon is falling
    as the prophecy spoke
And it's obvious to all
    God's children who are woke

YOU ARE MORE TO ME

On this quiet night
    Thanking You for all that You have given me
More than just Your life
    More than knowing that You have risen from the dead
I call You my Savior – You call me Your child

But You are more to me
    You are more than just a man and never-ending friend
You have given me
    Sight to see beyond the dullness of life that I was living
I call You my Father – You call me Your son

But You are more to me – so much more
And when I hear Your voice
And walk through Heaven's door
You'll even be much more to me
So much more
For I'll be Your servant
And You'll be much more

When I'm on my knees
    Sometimes I feel that You are far away – too far to hear my prayers
Then You comfort me
    You reach down into my heart and let me know You're here
I call You my shepherd – You call me Your sheep

But You are more to me
    When the world around me crumbles You're here to bear the weight
Standing next to me
    I feel You carry me when pressures of this life become too great
I call You the Great I Am – You call me Your bride

But You are more to me – so much more
And when I hear Your voice
And walk through Heaven's door
You'll even be much more to me
So much more
For I'll be Your servant
And You'll be much more

IT BEFUDDLES ME

It befuddles me
   to no end
When God is blamed
   for the bad on this earth
And never gets credit
   for the good that happens
It truly befuddles me

MERCY OVER JUDGMENT

If given a difficult decision,
I will always err on the side of mercy.
For the Scriptures say,
"Those who are merciful,
will be shown mercy."
Mercy is more powerful
than judgment.

MY GOD, MY GOD, WHY?

My God, my God, why in this country
    have so many forsaken you?
They have trampled over Your Grace
    they have perverted Your truth
They have sought out Your blessings
    they have embraced prosperity
While neglecting Your Word
    and disregarding the prophecies
All the poor needy children
    and parents they have shunned
While they stand so proudly
    having outlawed abortion
Yes, they feel so victorious
    in all they have achieved
As they elect the false prophet
    and worship him with bent knee
There are so many among us
    that call You their Lord
But they are blind with deception
    in praising hate and discord
A sad state of sorrow
    weighs heavy on my heart
As the church boasts so proudly
    for having played such a part

In supporting the beast
	You warned us would come
To deceive those not grounded
	in the truths of Your Son
Shout it from the rooftops
	proclaim it for all to hear
All that is happening today
	Is in Your Word so clear
Your plan will surely come to pass
	Your will on earth be done
The prophecies will be fulfilled
	and so ends this creation

CHRIST IN YOU

Lord through my struggles
    Of sin and despair
I searched through Your Word
    To find comfort there
But it seemed victory
    Was so far away
Then you broke through
    You showed me the way

Christ in you – the hope of glory
Dying to self – so you can be free
That He become greater
    As you become less
Is where you will find
    Peace and eternal rest

So, simple's the truth
    So great is the Lord
To see His face
    My greatest reward
If I never have
    More than Jesus in me
I'll have all I want
    For He's all I need

Father, forgive me
    For denying Your Son
The honor that's His
    For the work He's done
I've tried in my flesh
    To live righteously
Now gladly I die
    So, He can reign in me

Christ in you – the hope of glory
Dying to self – so you can be free
That He become greater
    As you become less
Is where you will find
    Peace and eternal rest

DEAR GOD

Dear God, what are You
    looking for?
You know I believe
    and so much more
You know that my faith
    rests solely in You
You know I seek only
    to know Your truth
Just how much more faith
    must I have right now
To move all these mountains
    please tell me, just how?
How much more faith
    do I possibly need
To cast all my troubles
    into the sea?
Just how much more
    do you want from me,
Before you respond
    to my deepest hearts need?
Just how much more?
    God, I just do not know,
Until You will honor
    these seeds that I sow

DEATH TO SELFISHNESS

Lord let me die
    to my selfish ways
So that Jesus
    can live through me

And do what's right
    the rest of my days
Until I see Your face
    in eternity

WATCHING THE TIME
(SONG OF A SELF-RIGHTEOUS FOOL)

Sitting in my pew the views just fine
Watching the time
Thoughts of mansions made of gold do shine
Watching the time
Oh, the world is going to hell
But I'm doing swell

Waiting for the train to pick me up
Watching the time
Pass the loaf of bread and fill my cup
Watching the time
Oh, the little starving children
But eating's not a sin

Why do I have to do what They say
My way will get me by
I give my ten and bow my head to pray
Watching the time

Had lunch with pastor and his wife today
Watching the time
Slipped him a few bucks to pave my way
Watching the time
Oh, the poor they're always with us
Uncle Sam has them a bus

Getting ready for the Lord to come
Watching the time
I'm paying for Their work to be all done
Watching the time
So, when I stand at those pearly gates
I won't have to wait

Why do I have to do what They say
My way will get me by
I give my ten and bow my head to pray
Watching the time

JOHN 1 (ALMIGHTY)

In the beginning was the Word
    The Word was with God, God He was
Through Him all creation was made
    Without Him nothing was shaped
In Him was life that became light
    For man in darkness to gain sight
The darkness could not understand
    The pureness of this sinless man

For He is Almighty
He is Almighty
Jesus is Almighty

There came a man so sent from God
    To testify about the Son
Through this light, men might believe
    Open their hearts they may receive
Though He came into the world
    And though He'd made the heavens and earth
Man could not recognize Him
    Until they turned from their own sin

For He is Almighty
He is Almighty
Jesus is Almighty

DON'T BE A HYPOCRITE

My belief and faith in God
are through the Gospel and
compassionate teachings
of Jesus Christ.
That is what I profess.
For me to waiver from,
contradict, or compromise
that truth
would make me a hypocrite.
BUT, I am not God.
The Scriptures say:
God is Just.
God is merciful
and will have mercy
on whom
They choose to have mercy on.
God and God ALONE
knows the motives
and true intentions
of a person's heart.
I am called to love
and not judge.
If you have
a relationship with God
through the Gospel of Jesus Christ,
DON'T BE A HYPOCRITE.
God does not need that
in these trying times.
God needs us
to be sincere, genuine, and love-
with the love of Jesus Christ.

AMONG THE TRYING FIRES

I come humbly to You Lord
   So foolish I have been
It seems I never learn from my mistakes
And when it seems I can't go on
   I can't lift up my head
You come and fill my heart with Holy Grace

And as tears flow from my eyes
   Gently reaching down
You lift me up and stand me on my feet
You speak Your words I hold so close
   And then You let me know
By opening my eyes so I can see

Father – break this heart of mine
   Pour Your love inside
I want to stand righteous before Your eyes
Don't – let my self give way - To my sinful desires
Lord – let this man stand with You - Among the trying fires

My goal is to be as Your Son
   By letting Him become
Conformed in me by dying to myself
To seek Your kingdom that has come
   So, we can be as one
So, Jesus will be all that there is left

Now let me seek to know Him
    And all His suffering
Let Jesus reign as Lord of my whole life
So, when I stand before Your throne
    All the flesh will burn
And I'll stand holy, pure within Your sight

Father – break this heart of mine
    Pour Your love inside
I want to stand righteous before Your eyes
Don't – let my self give way - To my sinful desires
Lord – let this man stand with You - Among the trying fires

KNOWLEDGE IS NOT POWER

Knowledge is not power.
Knowledge is the accumulation of
information in your brain.
What if the information is
faulty or lies?
What good is that knowledge?
Knowledge, in itself, is useless.
To make knowledge useful to all,
it must come with understanding.
Understanding takes knowledge
and uses it in a logical
and rational manner.
With understanding comes
the benefit of discernment.
Discernment gives us the ability
to separate the truth from the lie.
Knowledge used with understanding
and discernment is good.
But the greatest of all intellect
comes from our loving God.
Yes, wisdom from God is power.
NOT the wisdom of this world.

"For the wisdom of this world is foolishness in God's sight." (1)
For wisdom from God:
Will, "Love the Lord your God with all your heart and
	with all your soul and with all your might." (2)
Will, "Love your neighbor as yourself." (3)
Will, "Do to others as you would have them do to you." (4)
Will possess, "Love, joy, peace, patience, kindness, generosity,
	faithfulness, gentleness, and self-control." (5)
The wisdom from God IS POWER.

1. 1 Corinthians 3:19a NIV
2. Deuteronomy 6:5
3. Leviticus 19:18
4. Matthew 7:12
5. Galatians 5:22-23

GIVE US THE HEART

The prophecy's been spoken
    The Spirit's here for us
We're called to do Your work oh God
    But instead, we hate and fuss
The minutes, they grow shorter
    The hours have run down
It's time to lay the flesh aside
    And spread Your love around

Oh Lord our God – give us the heart
To reach the lost, the blind, the maimed
Give us the strength – to love the ones
That cause You hurt and hate Your name
Purge out the pride – destroy the walls
That keep Your light from shining down
Give us Your truth – to set us free
And save the world – for Your glory

Too many years we've wandered round
    In circles foolishly
While the world has turned to idol sin
    And Your heart has been so grieved
I pray we turn from selfish ways
    Open up our eyes to see
Love You, oh God, with all our heart
    And our neighbors selflessly

Oh Lord our God – give us the heart
To reach the lost, the blind, the maimed
Give us the strength – to love the ones
That cause You hurt and hate Your name
Purge out the pride – tear down the walls
That keep Your light from shining down
Give us Your truth – to set us free
And save the world – for Your glory

WHY THEY BELIEVE THE LIES

* The coming of the lawless one will be in accordance with how Satan
works. He will use all sorts of displays of power through signs and wonders
that serve the lie, and all the ways that wickedness deceives those who are
perishing. They perish because they refused to love the truth and so be
saved. For this reason God sends them a powerful delusion so that they
will believe the lie and so that all will be condemned who have not believed
the truth but have delighted in wickedness.   2 Thessalonians 2:9-12 NIV

No need to wonder
    why they believe the lies
It is all right here*
    where the truth abides

They chose not to listen
    to the truth within
So, God sends them delusions
    to justify their sins

No need to confront them
    they've made their choice
To believe all the lies
    to accept all the noise

God loves them still
    though they've chosen their path
And in eternal damnation
    they will pay for their past

I WISH

I wish I could take
    what I understand
Write it all down
    in words by my hand
So that you could see
    all that I know
Then maybe you'd believe
    what I've written is so
But it takes more than words
    written oh so right
For you to believe
    what's not in plain sight
All I can do now
    is speak truth I know
Pray you will listen
    and allow faith to grow
All that it takes
    is eyes that can see
Ears that will listen
    and a heart to believe

I BELIEVE

I believe
in God the Creator, the Beloved, and the Presence.
One deity comprised of three spirit entities.
I believe the Creator sent the Beloved to this earth
as the Messiah, Jesus Christ for the salvation of all people.
I believe Jesus Christ was born to the virgin Mary
by the Presence of the Holy Spirit.
I believe that Jesus Christ walked this earth, gave us the Word,
died on the cross, and rose from the dead for
our salvation, redemption, and justification, if we believe.
I believe Jesus Christ rose from the dead and walked the earth
for forty days appearing to the disciples and many others,
teaching them and instructing them to wait upon
the Presence of the Holy Spirit.
I believe that Jesus Christ then ascended back into heaven
to return to the side of the Creator,
at which time the Creator poured out the Presence
of the Holy Spirit upon all people who believe
from that time forth, according to the prophecy stated
in the Book of Joel.
I believe that the Presence of the Holy Spirit is
our guide, our counselor, and our comforter.
I believe that all people who call upon the name of Jesus Christ,
confess their sins, obey the Word, and do what is right
in the eyes of God will be saved.
I believe that, one day, Jesus Christ will return to this earth
and gather all who believe both from the dead and the living,
and provide us a new home where we will abide in the company
of God the Creator, the Beloved, and the Presence for all eternity.